The Power of Positive Living

John R. Bisagno

Gateway Seminary Library

BROADMAN PRESS
Nashville, Tennessee

BV
4510.2
.B57
1969

© Copyright 1969 • Broadman Press
All rights reserved

Fourth Printing

4219-10

ISBN: 0-8054-1910-1

Dewey Decimal classification number: 248.4
Library of Congress catalog card number: 70-93913
Printed in the United States of America

3.S7118

Contents

1. A Positive Sense of Need 7
2. A Positive Conversion 19
3. A Positive Beginning 29
4. A Positive Attitude 40
5. A Positive Mind 45
6. A Positive Witness 53

1

A Positive Sense of Need

On the night of April 5, 1934, in Augusta, Kansas, a seven-pound, screaming bundle of nervous energy was born. It was me! My parents, Jay and Clair Reece Bisagno, were always good people, conscientious Christians since Junior age. I went to Sunday School and church only when I had to because, since I was not a Christian, it meant little to me. When I was thirteen years of age, I joined the church and signed a card and was immersed in a baptistry, but nothing happened.

One afternoon, I came home from school and heard my sister practicing her baritone horn. I watched for a little while and said, "Here! Let me see that thing for a minute." She gave it to me and I began to play. I can honestly say it was one of the easiest things I ever did.

Music came natural to me. I just picked it up and

played. After about five or ten minutes I picked out, by ear, a popular tune of the day, "Pistol Packin' Mama."

A few days later, my father came home from the city sporting a thirty-five-dollar, slightly beat-up, used trumpet. I began to practice and soon picked out the scales and a few popular songs.

Shortly thereafter, my parents moved from Bentley, Kansas, to Perry, Oklahoma, where I enrolled in Perry High School as a freshman. I joined the high school band, and learned, much to my dismay, that there were fourteen trumpet players and I was number fourteen. I quickly moved up to first chair and remained there the next four years.

Toward the end of my freshman year, as a fourteen-year-old boy, after I had been playing about six or eight months, the high school band began to prepare for a summer concert. About twice every summer, the band played an open-air, free concert in the park, much to the enjoyment of all the townspeople. This particular concert was to be of the popular variety, mostly jazz numbers. I'll never forget it. It was my first big solo. Being the first chair trumpet player, I had all the trumpet solos. It could either be played from the music or strictly by jamming, which means that the soloist knows the chord progression and plays the melody just as he feels it. That night, I was really feeling it.

This was my first big night. As the drummer started

the syncopated beats to the introduction, I stood and began to play. The beat pounded in my blood, a spotlight beamed in my eyes, the music filled my heart, and I was thrilled as I had never been before. When I finished that "hot ride," I sat down amid deafening applause. The people applauded until I played it again and again. The concert was soon over and they began to gather around. This was my first big night, to thrill to the applause of men and to feel the drive of the jazz beat in my blood. I loved every minute of it. After the concert, a young fellow came up to me and said, "Johnny, I have a Western swing band that plays at the American Legion Hall in Billings, Oklahoma, every Saturday night. We play three hours and you will make about $15.00. There will be about four hundred people there, many of them teen-agers. Will you go?"

"Sure," I said. "Why not?" I grabbed at it, and started down a road which, for many, has been a road of no return.

I quickly found popularity, and began running with a fast crowd and living high. It wasn't long until the offers started coming. Before I was out of high school, I had done one-nighters with Herschel Clotheir, Hank Thompson, Merle Lindsay, Leon McAuliffe, Johnnie Lee Wills, Bob Willis; and before I finished my freshman year in college, I had sat in with Ray Anthony, Woody Herman, and other name bands, and made more money in one night than most kids made in three months.

Then something strange began to happen. I found that no matter how you try to live, when you associate with that kind of life, you either must give in and do what the crowd does, or be laughed at and get out. I took the easy way and went along with the crowd. I have given my testimony all over the country, and time and time again they have come to me and said, "Johnny, it is just like you said. It started on the dance floor. I thought I had to be popular. I thought I had to go along with the crowd. I didn't want to be a wallflower. Then it was the wrong crowd, then it was the parked automobile, and now, my life is wrecked and I'm only fourteen or fifteen years old."

Take the words of somebody who has been over the path. You play with fire and you are going to get burned. You take the primary, basic, physical attraction out of the modern-day dance and you will have no dance. Nobody told me these things. I didn't read it in a book. I experienced it. If it is not so, why don't boys dance with boys, and girls with girls?

So, with no moral standard to speak of, I began to do what the gang did, go where they went, say what they said, act as they acted, and because of the thrill of it and the desire to be popular, I had no time for God. The theme song of hell is, "Everybody's Doing It." Anyone can go along with the crowd. I'd rather dare to be different. Sure they will laugh at you, sure they will make fun of you, sure they will call you narrow and religious. God asks only that you turn your back on self and sin, and live for him. That is the least you can do—live for him who died for you.

When I served the devil, I made him a good hand, but when I decided that I was going to serve Jesus Christ, I vowed that I was going to make him a good hand; none of this halfhearted, wishy-washy stuff for me. It is not easy to be a real Christian. Don't say it is any bed of roses. Take up your cross, and follow Jesus. Christ said, "If you are not willing to forsake your mother and father and loved ones, and even your own self, you are not worthy to be my disciple." The apostle Paul, writing to young Timothy, said, "Endure hardness, as a good soldier of Jesus Christ." It is no easy job to be a Christian, but I will guarantee you one thing: you live all the way for my Saviour—not 99 percent of the way but all the way—and I won't guarantee you an easy time, but I promise you such happiness as you've never known. It may not always look like it, but you will be on the winning side in the end.

In 1951, I enrolled at Oklahoma State University and joined the Kappa Sigma Fraternity and announced I was going to start a dance band. "Why, Man," they said, "you're crazy! There are already four bands over here and they are big orchestras. They've got the dance work sewed up. You're just an unknown freshman. You won't get to first base. This is a big school," and on and on. But I wouldn't be discouraged. I had gone to college to start a jazz band, to make money with a jazz band, and make a name for myself, and that was just what I was going to do.

All the bands were the big orchestras with the fancy tuxedoes and special arrangements. I saw my chance and went to town. I organized six musicians—not college boys, but professional musicians. My men had played with Clyde McCoy, Blue Barron, the Firehouse Five Plus Two, and several others. Although I was seventeen, they were not college kids, they were men, they were professional musicians. They had families to support, but they worked for me.

By the end of the first semester, the students gave us the name of "Aggieland's Number One Dance Band." The first sorority dance we played for was the Kappa Delta Christmas Dance. They came in their formals and their tuxedoes for a nice, quiet evening of ballroom dancing. But, when my boys stood up the first night, and started playing, they went crazy. I mean they went crazy! The ties came off and some of the shoes, and they began to dance to a new beat they had never heard before. I was in the height of my glory.

In a few weeks my name was spread across the campus on posters, in newspapers, and magazines. I could have anything I wanted and I could get away with anything I wanted to. I had popularity, a name, friends, anything a teen-age boy's heart desired. I had it and I loved every minute of it. The other fraternities and sororities heard about our band, and by the end of the year, we had played for twenty-one of the twenty-seven fraternity and sorority dances on the campus. The fellows in my band made twelve to fifteen dollars a night. I was making from seventy-five to one hundred and fifty dollars a night. I didn't study much, but made good grades. I maintained a B average throughout my freshman year in college. Smart, you say? No! In some colleges the tests have been the same for years. Many a night before an exam I have paid one of my friends to get those answers for me. I would write them out, turn them in before the test was given, and go off somewhere and play for a dance. I didn't care what it cost me.

One night the Oklahoma Aggies won their five hundredth basketball game. The students went wild and had a big walkout, and the college declared a day of celebration. I saw a chance to make some quick money. I rented the Student Union ballroom for $100.00 and threw a big Victory Dance. Twenty-seven hundred kids of the seven thousand on the campus came to that dance. They paid plenty to get in, and after I paid for the hall, paid the boys a guaranteed amount, and pocketed what was left, I was a long way from broke.

The next summer, I joined a Dixieland band out of New Orleans and traveled till August. During that summer, I got my first real taste of full-time traveling in the show business world, and, believe me, it was an ungodly mess. These were not kids, this was not a high school dance, this was the "real McCoy." This was where my desire for a thrill, fame, and the big time had taken me, and it was not a pretty picture.

We did a lot of one-night stands, traveling often four and five hundred miles a night, arriving in a town just in time to clean up, set up, and play; then, shove off for the next dance job. Believe me, the three or four hours of thrill you get is not worth the twenty hours of torment that one has to go through, and there is plenty of it. It is as artificial as a paper moon! It is a thrill that passes away. It is an escape that doesn't satisfy.

One night that summer, with its glitter and glamor, thrill of professional night-clubbing, and entertaining, I realized there was something missing. Many were the nights I've gone back to my hotel room after playing a job from nine until two, jamming from three until six in the morning, and laid down on a bed and watched that ceiling start swimming around, and I've asked myself, "Is it really worth it?" The last engagement that summer was at the Officer's Club of the Craig Air Force Base, Selma, Alabama. We drank, caroused, cursed, smoked, and played, night after night. The band had been traveling and we were all tired.

On the night of July 28, 1952 I packed my trumpet and left what was to be the last dance I ever played. The band broke up, temporarily, for a two weeks' vacation. I was to rejoin the boys for our next engagement that started two weeks later in Omaha, Nebraska. I said good-by and left for a two weeks' vacation at my hometown, Perry, Oklahoma, with my folks. That was some vacation. It's lasted for years now, and will keep

A Positive Sense of Need 15

on lasting until I lay down my cross at Jesus' feet; and then, as a matter of fact, that vacation will really just begin. Here's how it happened. . . .

I left Selma about 12:00 on a Monday night, my pockets filled with money, my suitcase packed, anxious to go home for a little rest. I arrived in Oklahoma City about 11:00 the next night and got a bus up to Perry. When I got there at 2:30 A.M. and went to my home, I was surprised to find I couldn't get in. After I knocked and knocked, and tried all the windows, I decided my parents must be gone. So, I went downtown and spent the night in a hotel.

The next morning I got up bright and early—about noon, which was early for me—and went over to my parents' place of business. I learned that they were in California at a convention. I decided the only thing for me to do was to go on to Omaha, find a nice apartment, check in and meet some friends, paint the town red for a few days, and wait for the band. I started to the bus station to catch a bus for Omaha. As I walked down the north side of the square, a fellow came up to me and said, "Hi, Johnny, what are you doing home?" He was the pastor of the First Baptist Church.

"Hi, preacher," I said. "Just here a couple of days to visit."

"Well," he said, "since you've got some time off, why don't you come spend a few days at Falls Creek." Falls Creek Baptist Assembly is the world's largest youth encampment. Every year, twenty to thirty thousand teen-agers come to Falls Creek, in the Arbuckle Mountains of Davis, Oklahoma. They have great recreation, classes in the morning, and two preaching services a day—the last place I wanted to go.

"Who? Me?" I said. "Me? Go down there with all those sissified Christian kids? Man, they're not my speed."

"But, Johnny," he said, "a lot of those kids down there know you. They've heard you play. They've listened to you on the radio. They've been to your dances. Why, you could go down there and really have a time."

He blew my head up bigger and bigger. My eyes lit up and I said, "Yeah! That's not such a bad idea. You know, I could go down there and really have myself one good time." Now I didn't tell him this, but I decided I could go and really tear up Falls Creek, meet some new chicks, cat around with the boys, start some jam sessions, and really strut my stuff with all those religious fanatics. The devil gave me some bright ideas, but the Lord had other plans.

I said, "Okay, preacher, I'll see you there." I went home, got my car and left for Falls Creek. I was really going to show off and have myself one big time. I drove into Falls Creek, rolled my windows down, honked the horn, took a few bows, and said, "Yes, sir, folks, here he is, ole 'Hot Lips' in person. Get your eyes full, here I am, all you lucky people."

Well, I went to the cabin and, because it was compulsory, went to the service that night. I sat on the back row, and took it all in. I had never seen anything like it. There were thousands in the tabernacle that hot, stuffy, July night, and they had all come to see me, so I tried to tell myself. Then it started. First, the song leader jumped up and down and waved his arms like an eagle about to fly. What? I thought, no dancing girls? No brass band? What kind of a crazy club is this, anyway? I had the time of my life. I looked at the preacher and said, "Good heavens. I wouldn't be one of those crazy things for a million dollars a week." And now, I would do it for nothing!

Well, I went to the cabin, went to sleep, and the next morning set out to do what I wanted to do. I went over to the Enid cabin where I knew a lot of boys from high school band days and persuaded some of them to have a jam session with me. We got out in the front yard, on the main corner of Falls Creek, and started going to town. In five minutes, hundreds of kids gathered around and were clapping their hands and tapping their feet and hollering, "Crazy man, go man go," and some of them even started jitterbugging. Well, it wasn't five more minutes till the guards came and broke it up.

I didn't mind, it had made me popular. Everyone knew I was there. I had done what I came to do—show off and have a big time tearing up Falls Creek with a jam session. I was proud of myself. So, I went to the cabin and got ready to go to church.

This time, I sat on the back row again, and looked around, not so much with a feeling of hilarity, but with a feeling of disgust. I felt I was better than everyone else. I began to criticize. I listened for bad notes, mistakes, flat singing, and dulness of the program. I didn't listen to the sermon. The next morning, I packed and prepared to leave. I loaded my car and got in, but I just couldn't leave.

2

A Positive Conversion

I didn't know why, but somehow I couldn't get away from Falls Creek. So, I got out of my car and started to walk. I walked until three o'clock. I wasn't going anywhere, just walking and trying to find myself. I must have walked five or six miles up and down those Arbuckle Mountains that day, before I stopped. Seated nearby were three teen-aged couples, three boys and three girls. They had their shoes off, sitting around in a circle, holding hands and singing. Just then, the Lord spoke to me. "Now, look at you, with all your dance bands, with all your girl friends, with all your fair-weather pals, with all your clothes, popularity, money, good times, with the sparkle, the show, the glitter and the glamor of it all, you're just as miserable as a man can be. Look at those kids down there. They've never led a band. They've never stood before thousands of people and thrilled to their applause.

They've never had the popularity you've had. They've never been to the places you've been, or done the things you've done, but those kids are happy. They have something you don't have."

I said to myself, "Boy, you've been played for a fool: all this time you've been barking up the wrong tree. You've been doing the wrong thing to try to find happiness." I got the answer from God. I said to myself, "If that is the answer to this pressure, this unrest, then it's for me. I don't know what those kids have, but I mean to find out, and no matter what it costs, I'm going to get it." When I said that, when I made up my mind to seek what I had seen in the lives of those kids that afternoon, the burden left. I smiled all of a sudden, just as if someone had taken the world off my shoulders. I stood to my feet and started walking back towards the camp. For the first time in years, I was genuinely happy.

I was not saved until that night, but when I made up my mind to seek what the Lord had for me, when I started toward the cross, God came along and gave me a hand. That night I went to church again. The preacher began to say, "I want you kids to listen to me, and I want you to listen closely. I am disgusted with what I have seen here at Falls Creek the last few days. Every night I've preached and given an invitation, and four or five hundred of you have come down these aisles, chomping your gum forty whacks a second, and bawling your eyes out, saying, 'I want to rededi-

A Positive Conversion

cate my life, get right with Jesus, and quit this and quit that,' and the next day I see you out doing the same things, saying the same things, dressing the same way, acting the same way."

He said, "I'm sick and tired of this shallow dedication. I'm going to give an invitation that is going to be the hardest I have ever given. I don't care if one comes, I don't care if just ten come, I want those ten to mean business."

He continued, "I want you to think straight and seriously. If you are going to go on living the same way, hold on to those seats with all you've got and don't you budge. I don't want you to make a fool out of yourself and me and my Saviour tonight. I don't want any music, I don't want any singing, I don't want any standing. But, if you can say—'Preacher, the best I know how, from this night on, I'll be different, from this night on, I'll stand true to Jesus Christ. I'll leave everything for him. I don't care what the crowd says. I don't care what they do. I'm going to live a godly, separated, dedicated, Christian life'—I want you to come down this aisle with everybody looking at you and stand at the front."

He was right. Not many came. Maybe thirty or forty. I said to myself, Preacher, I'm just enough of a man to accept your challenge. Brother, you're talking my language. You've got yourself a hand. There were thousands there that night, but John Bisagno, the trumpet player from Perry, was the first one down the aisle. There were not many of us, but I'll never forget the preacher's words, "I don't care how few come tonight, I want you few to mean business." I did. That night Jesus came into my heart and called me to be an evangelistic singer.

The next morning, August 2, 1952, I sent telegrams to the boys in the band and canceled all my contracts.

One afternoon I happened to be at Oklahoma State and overheard some of the other boys in the campus hangout saying, "Say, have you heard that ole 'Hot Lips' Bisagno has gone down there to that religious school and got religion? Brother, if that is not a laugh! He'll last about two weeks there and then he'll be right back up here at every nightclub playing again. Why, they're so fanatic down there—they don't even dance. What's old Hot Lips going to do?" I turned away quickly, gritting my teeth and praying a little, "Lord, if you ever helped me, help me now." And, imbedded on my mind, once again came that scene, and I heard those words, "I don't care if one comes tonight, I want that one to mean business." And I said to myself, "Lord, I'll be that one."

Now the devil knew I loved jazz, and he knew I had it in my soul and in my blood and he made it plenty tough on me. Many is the time I've gone to my room at night, those first couple of weeks at Oklahoma Baptist University, and turned on the radio to hear the words, "From the beautiful Parisian Room in the Hotel Roosevelt, downtown New Orleans, Louisiana, it's the music of Tony Almerico and his Dixieland All-Stars." I would hear them kick off that theme song, "Way Down Yonder in New Orleans," and my heart would turn over, a lump would come in my throat, and the blood in my veins would start pounding with that beat, and I would have to turn away and turn it off quickly. The words of my conscience kept coming up to my ear, "What's it going to be, Johnny, jazz or Jesus?" and I started to go back. Then, somehow, Jesus always won.

My first month at Oklahoma Baptist University was rather unhappy. I wasn't making too many friends because I was so much out of place. Occasionally I would slip and curse. Once in a while I'd get to jazzing up the music in the band, once in a while I forgot. I was a new Christian, it was tough, really tough. Some of the kids tried to help me, some ridiculed and made fun—Christian kids, I'm sorry to say—but they didn't understand.

One Tuesday I sat in a noonday service and heard a young fellow by the name of Paul McCray preaching. I had been a little disheartened at some of the wishy-washy Pharisaism I'd seen on the campus, but he wasn't like that. He preached hard. He really challenged the kids, and I liked it. I liked his fire and enthusiasm. I went up to him after it was over and said, "Hi, Buddy, what are you going to do when you get out of school?"

He said, "I'm going to be an evangelist. I'm an evangelist now."

I said, "Well, what do you know about that! I'm going to be an evangelistic song leader. Let's team up and set the world on fire."

"All right," he said, "I'm holding a revival Friday night for three days in the Immanuel Baptist Church of Pryor, Oklahoma. You can be the song leader."

"Okay," I said, "I'll be there."

That Friday night, as we were about thirty minutes out of Pryor, the thought hit me: I wonder what they do in revivals? I had seen a couple of guys lead the singing in school, but I had just been converted about three weeks before and I really didn't know what I was going to do or what I was supposed to do. I was in a jam. I walked out on the platform and said, "Well, here goes nothing." And believe me, there went nothing.

I sat down on the platform, and Paul said, "Now John Bisagno, converted dance-band leader, will come lead our song service." I picked up my trumpet, raised it high, and played a couple of hot licks. Then, I stuck it down between my legs and started clapping my hands and said, "Come on, all you cats, let's stand and hit it with 'Amazing Grace.'"

I didn't look, but I expect that Paul crawled under the back seat about that time, and if I had had good sense I would have done the same thing. Well, we managed to struggle through that slightly jazzy song service, and before the three nights were over, God had given us two Oklahoma Baptist University preacher

A Positive Conversion

boys forty-three conversions in that small church.

During the next several years, I married, conducted hundreds of revivals, and joined the Hyman Appelman evangelistic team as associate evangelist.

In 1959, we went to the British Isles for three months of evangelizing. While in Belfast, Ireland, God began to deal with me regarding the call to preach. We were in a strange country with no financial security and hesitated much, but eventually surrendered to do his will completely. Since that time it has been my privilege to cover the fifty states proclaiming the glorious gospel of Christ. Jesus said, "I am come that they might have life, and that they might have it more abundantly," and to serve him, to preach his Word, to be his own, is the greatest thrill the world can know.

In 1965, I became pastor of the First Southern Baptist Church in Del City, Oklahoma. God has blessed us since with an average of eighteen conversions and additions every Sunday. I believe it is the greatest church in the world.

Between April, 1947, and August, 1952, I played for a lot of dances, danced with a lot of girls, drank with a lot of boys, told a lot of jokes, saw a lot of sights, had a lot of thrills, and lived a lot of life. I was on my way to the top for myself and didn't care too much how I got there as long as I got what I wanted. I've been around. I've had what the devil can offer. I've had what men could offer. I've had what I could get for myself. But when I came to Jesus Christ and turned it all over to him, I found out what living really is.

I've played "Stardust" before thousands. I've played "Onward Christian Soldiers" and preached before even greater thousands. I am a testimony of what the Son of God can do in a life. If you want to have a good time for yourself, seek the pleasures of the world—that is strictly your choice. Take the word of one who knows, though, it doesn't pay. If you want to live for Jesus Christ, sell out completely to him, turn your life and testimony, all you've ever been and ever hope to be, over to him and let him make out of you what he will. I can promise you no bed of roses, but a thrill, the likes of which you have never known.

If you don't hear or read or understand another word I've said, I hope you will understand what I am going to say now.

Have you ever been thirsty, really thirsty, your lips cracking, your throat parched, your mouth dry? I have. Let's say that you are thirsty, and you want something to quench your thirst. Take a bottle of orange pop. Look at it, hold it up, doesn't it look good, isn't it alluring? See the frost dripping from the side! Look at it sparkle! See how bubbling and bright and effervescent it is! You can't wait to get it to your lips. You can't wait to thrill as it goes down your throat and you taste its sweet, refreshing flavor. It was so attractive, looked so good, and satisfied so well. But what about it? In two or three minutes, what happens?

A Positive Conversion

You are left with a sweet, sticky taste in your mouth, and with all its sparkle, color, and appeal, it doesn't satisfy. Pick it up again, now that it is empty. Look at it closely. Read the label. It was there all the time, you just didn't see it: artificially flavored, artificially colored, artificially sweetened.

The world is glamorous, alluring, and appealing, but look closely for a minute. It, too, is artificial. There is only one thing that will satisfy your thirst. Water!! Take a glass of water, drink it when you are thirsty. It is not sweet, doesn't sparkle, is not fancy, nor artificial. It is just pure, plain, unadulterated water, but it satisfies. It quenches your thirst.

Jesus said, "Come unto me, all ye that labour and are heavy laden, and I will give you rest." He says, "Are you thirsty? Are you tired of sin? Are you tired of the world with its artificial appeal?" Jesus said, "I am the water of life. Take of this bread that I give you and you will never be hungry again. Take of this water that I give you and you will never thirst again."

Nothing but water will really satisfy thirst. Nothing but the Water of life, Jesus Christ, can satisfy the thirst of the soul that is ever present and desires to be satisfied. I'm not an old man. I'm a young man, but I saw God work a miracle in my life and I wouldn't trade one day of living for Jesus Christ for all the thrills the world has to offer in a lifetime. I tried him. I tried Jesus and he's wonderful. He really satisfies! As one of his representatives, I offer him to you. Won't you take him on my recommendation? You'll be glad you did.

3

A Positive Beginning

Positive living begins with positive beginnings, and that means Jesus in the heart of the child. But when is the best time for the child to be saved? The Mormons have set the conversion of children at age 8. The Jews at age 12. Many Baptists experience it far before then. It is unfortunate that so much controversy has arisen around the subject of childhood conversion. Never is the devil more pleased than when conversion is discouraged at any age. "Let them wait," some tell us. "Let them grow up." "We try to make men out of boys." Strange, for I find that Jesus tried to make boys out of men. Listen to the words of the Saviour, "Except ye be converted, and become as little children, ye shall not enter into the kingdom of heaven."

I wonder sometimes if the pride of the preacher is not involved. I fear we don't believe in children being saved because there is not as much to brag about.

Somehow it appeals to our ego to say, "We didn't catch many fish, but the ones we did catch were big."

I learned a long time ago, when you meet a fact in the road, it is better not to argue. Just take off your hat and say, "Howdy, Brother." You can argue until you are blue in the face, but the fact remains that the majority of people that have ever been saved in this old world were saved under age 12. The average age of the conversion of all Southern Baptist preachers is 9, and the average age of the conversion of all Southern Baptist foreign missionaries is 8. Strange, but true. The longer you wait, the less the chances. Little wonder the Saviour said, "Suffer the little children to come unto me." Today is the day of salvation.

Communist soldiers are said to walk into the schools of Havana and ask the children to pray to Jesus for candy. Of course, they get none. Then they will say, "Pray to Fidel Castro for candy," and candy is distributed among the children.

Condemned slayer Caryl Chessman said, "There was a time in my life between age 10 and 14 that I was a confused, bewildered boy. Someone could have reached me with the gospel, but nobody tried."

Psychologists tell us that what we are by age 5, we will become. I believe in childhood conversion for many reasons.

1. Jesus said so—that should be sufficient.
2. History proves that most are converted in childhood.

A Positive Beginning

3. God blesses the church that blesses children. In twelve years in the evangelistic field and seventeen years in the ministry, I have preached in nearly every conceivable kind of situation and have never seen it fail. The church that snubs the children, the church that ridicules their conversion, will find the Spirit of God grieved and few more results coming in a revival. But let a church rejoice when boys and girls are saved, and the Holy Spirit will bless and many more conversions will follow. Put it down, God blesses the church that blesses children.

4. I believe that children know what they are doing. It is most unfortunate that many uninformed adults are critical of children being converted. Who says that children don't know what they are doing? Preachers and others who make a study of it and give their life to it? Not at all. Those who make it their business to know what they are talking about readily adhere to the importance of childhood conversion. Now, while they are young. Today, while their hearts are sensitive, this is the time for conversion.

But if you have a sincere question as to whether children really understand, remember the simplicity of salvation. Isaiah described it as a highway where a wayfaring man, though a fool, need not err therein. What do you think children have to know to be saved? The same thing anyone else does, of course. Two things are required. Knowledge of sin, and faith. With a child, you need not worry about faith. To him, Jesus Christ is real. With adults, you must worry about faith. They must feel it, see it, understand it, touch it—everything but accept it in faith. You don't need to worry about an adult's knowledge of sin—he has plenty of that by experience. The only problem with children is not their faith, but their knowledge of sin. If they have that, they can be saved. Children today are gaining in a knowledge of sin, at a younger age than ever before. They are doing things in high school that used to go on in college. And in grade school, that they did only in high school. The devil is making the appeal of sin at an earlier age than at any time in the history of the world.

Just make sure that the child has a knowledge of sin and do not limit his faith. We allow him to have faith in everything else except this. You tell him that a great big fat man goes bouncing around the sky throwing presents down to all the little kids for Christmas. That is all right; you want him to believe it. You tell him that the Easter bunny comes hippety-hopping along, laying chocolate Easter eggs and that too is fine, because you want him to believe it. The preacher comes along and tells him that Jesus died for him and that he can be saved by asking Christ to come into his heart, and you say, *"No, you can't believe that—that's the truth."*

In reality, the truth is that the child's conversion might make his parent's own backslidden condition so obvious that it hurts, and he resents it. Oh, it is

A Positive Beginning

all right to believe in Santa Claus, the Easter bunny, Bat Man, and Superman, but you can't believe in Jesus. That makes me look bad, because I am so backslidden.

How unfortunate for parents. Jesus said that it would be better to have a millstone hanged about your neck and be drowned in the depths of the sea than to stand in the way and impede the spiritual progress of a child who wants to come to him. I wouldn't want to stand in your shoes on judgment day if you have refused to let your child be saved. Who are you to say the Holy Spirit cannot deal with one at a young age? Who are you to determine the teaching of the staff and teachers and the pleading of the Holy Spirit are all in vain and the time is not now? Woe again, I say unto you.

Oftentimes, people come forward as teen-agers and adults and say, "I want to be saved again." "I went forward when I was a child, but I didn't know what I was doing." When I see this happen, I question these people carefully. In 99 percent of the cases, I find that they did know what they were doing but that the person that dealt with them didn't know what he was doing. If we are too busy to kneel and pray with children and take time to lead them to Christ, if we are so high and mighty that all we can do is shake hands and sit them down, then God have mercy on us. We are filling our churches with unsaved people. Again I say, in most cases, it wasn't the child who didn't know what he was doing.

5. I believe in being saved while you are young because when you are older, you love sin and sin keeps you from Jesus. Don't tell me there is no pleasure in sin. There is a bang in sin. It is a great thrill, but it is temporary, it doesn't last, it is artificial. Why are the beer joints and the dives, the gambling joints, the dirty movies filled? Because there is pleasure in sin.

By the time young people are thirteen, fourteen, and fifteen, the devil is making sin appealing. He is making such a pitch for their young lives, that if you have not already won their allegiance to Jesus Christ, you'll not win many of them. If you think that isn't true, drive up and down the streets of your city at midnight. See them—thirteen, fourteen, fifteen, sixteen —in the back of cars, smoking, necking, throwing out beer cans, living like the devil.

Go to Sunday School? Go to church? Not them— that's kid stuff. Why, they're fifteen years old now, they've discovered America. What is the heart of it? Sin. They have tasted of the forbidden fruit, and they are not going to give it up for anybody. I am convinced that the real reason behind 99 percent of the men I can't win to Christ is simply one pet sin that nobody knows about, which they are not going to give up. The love of sin keeps people from Christ. Parents, believe me, the devil is lowering the age. He is making sin enticing, lower and lower and lower every year. We must win them to Jesus Christ now. By the time they are thirteen and fourteen, very few

A Positive Beginning

will leave the world for Jesus.

6. I believe in being saved when you are young because when you get older, pride increases. Pride keeps you from Christ. It really does. When I take my little boys a present, they are not going to care whether it is worth 5¢ or $10.00—they couldn't care less. But my little girl, at twelve, already knows how to look at the label and see if it is a brand name or not.

I daresay that the five-year-old son of the garbage collector in your city would think nothing of playing with the five-year-old son of the mayor. But I doubt seriously that the city officials and the garbage collector belong to the same clubs, the same churches, and live in the same neighborhood. I have seen children all over the world come down the aisle to Jesus Christ. Do you know how they respond? The same way. I have seen them in jungles of South America, I have seen them in Alaska, I have seen them in Canada and in Scotland. They all come alike.

Adults look at them and say that if they're not crying, they are not sincere. It's not that they aren't sincere—they're just not inhibited. They are just not full of pride. They just don't care what you think. They don't care if there are three or three thousand present. If they want to go to Jesus Christ, they are going to stand up and go. But adults will stand back and hang on to the pews until their knuckles turn white. "I can't do it," they say. "I can't humble myself. Not big, ole wonderful me. Get on my knees at that altar and say I am a sinner? No!" That's pride. Many adults are far too proud to come to Christ. Pride, pride, pride keeps men from Christ, and these boys and girls don't have that kind of pride yet. That is another reason why Jesus says, "Let the little children come unto me."

7. Then too, children don't hold grudges. I tried to win a man to Christ in a little country town in Oklahoma years ago, but couldn't. Leaning on his hoe handle between two rows of corn, he said, "Preacher, you want to know why I've never been saved?" I said, "I do." "Well," he continued, "I'll tell you. Seven years ago my neighbor's dog came on my yard and ate some pedigreed chickens I was raising for the county fair. I kicked him and ran him off. The neighbor came back, the dog came back, and I got my gun and shot and killed him—the dog, not the neighbor. We had an argument and haven't spoken for seven years. I don't come on his yard and he doesn't come on mine." He said, "Preacher, if I'm ever saved I'll have to apologize to that old boy, won't I?" I said, "You sure will." He replied, "I'll never do it." The reason? *Pride!!!*

Many churches in America are robbing themselves of blessings and stifling the Holy Spirit because of grudges. Nearly every church in America has some who don't sing in the choir anymore because they got their feelings hurt. There are some folks they just don't speak to. The Holy Spirit is grieved because of your grudges.

A Positive Beginning

But children don't hold grudges. Sometimes my little boys will be playing and get in a fuss. They will start banging each other over the head with their toys and you would think that World War III was on. Maybe five minutes later, I'll say, "Tony and Timmy, what on earth were you guys fighting about?" And they will say, "I don't know, Daddy, I don't know." They forgot. You see, children don't hold grudges. But adults do!!

8. I believe in children being saved because they have no preconceived ideas that have to be changed. Children don't have any excuses. Come now, how often have you ever heard a ten-year-old boy say, "Ain't got the feeling yet—don't push me, when my time comes, I'll know it"? Have you ever heard a little twelve-year-old say, "I'm too mean"? Did you ever hear an eight-year-old say, "There is too much to give up"? No, but adults come up with those soul-damning excuses that are keeping many from coming to Christ. Children don't have any preconceived ideas—no excuses.

I go out soul-winning several hours a week. Ten percent of my time is spent in *how* and ninety percent in *why*. Right, preachers? We spend very little of our time explaining how to be saved, most of it is answering a lot of excuses. I have never met a boy or girl that has been to Sunday School a dozen times in his life that you could not sit down with, without emotion or pressure, and win to Jesus Christ in five minutes.

Never have I seen that.

Boys and girls, if you go on unconverted, you go on without Jesus. The love of sin, grudges, pride, envy, gossip, hatred, excuses, all of these things like roadblocks will stack up against you. For many of you, it may never be possible for you to come to salvation, staggering through the maze of doubts and excuses and problems and reasons the devil will multiply on your path. I urge you, as simply as I know how, and yet, as fervently as I would to a group of condemned men in a penitentiary, to repent of your sins, to receive Jesus Christ as your Saviour. I plead with you mothers and dads to open your hearts to the Master's voice and allow, yea, encourage your youngster to come to the Master.

9. Let the children come to the Saviour that they might give their whole life to Jesus. Space forbids me to tell of the great men, such as George W. Truett, who, saved at a young age, gave not a half, but a whole life to him. "Only one life, 'twill soon be past. Only what's done for Christ will last."

I recently finished a tour of evangelistic campaigns in South America sponsored by the Foreign Mission Board of the Southern Baptist Convention. There were thirteen of us down there on the team. All of them were converted from five-and-a-half to seven-and-a-half years of age, except me, and I was eighteen when I was saved. They *can* be saved as children, and in the great majority of cases, they must be or they never will.

A Positive Beginning

Too Little

Said a precious little laddie, to his father one day,
"May I give my heart to Jesus, let Him wash my sins away?"

"Oh, my son, but you're too little, wait until you older grow,
Bigger folk, 'tis true, need Jesus, but little ones are safe, you know."

Said the father to his laddie, as a storm was coming on,
"Are the sheep all safely sheltered, safe within the fold, my son?"

"All the big ones are, my father, but the lambs, I let them go,
For I didn't think it mattered; little ones are safe, you know."

Oh, my Brother! Oh, my Sister! Have you too made that mistake?
Little hearts that now are yielding, may be hardened then—Too Late.

E're the evil days come nigh them, "Let the children come to me,
And forbid them not," said Jesus, "For of such shall my Kingdom be."

4

A Positive Attitude

Great people discuss ideas. Average people discuss things. Little people discuss other people. Through the years, I have found it nearly impossible to get great men to discuss the faults of other people. The critic spends most of his time studying other people's faults, shortcomings, and failures, probably because he is so unable to cope with his own problems that he finds security in the defense that there are others who share his inadequacies.

The perplexity with which one views the critic is compounded when he recognizes that the critic, either by inference or direct statement, infers that he has the solution to the problems of others. Yet the very fact that he is critical points out that he has made a miserable mess out of his own life. If the blind be leaders of the blind, they shall both fall into the ditch.

Let us consider why criticism is dangerous, why peo-

A Positive Attitude

ple criticize, and how to deal with the problem of criticism. May the Spirit of God give us insight into this, one of Christendom's most awful and obvious sins.

Criticism is dangerous because of its source. The critical always hurt themselves. They cry "Wolf-Wolf" so long that they're seldom believed. "Well, consider the source," is a just obituary of most critics. We never do quite as much harm to ourselves as when we criticize other people. Criticism is dangerous because the entire truth is seldom, if ever, told. If I have learned anything from dealing with the problems of people, it is that there are always two sides to every story.

The whole truth never known is usually less dangerous than half the truth often told. The criticized person seldom, if ever, has an opportunity to tell his side. The Bible tells us if a brother is overtaken with a fault, he is to be restored by one who is spiritual. If you have any concern about the one you are criticizing, then you will go to that one and talk to him and try to help him. Otherwise, your interest is only selfish and hypocritical.

Psychologists tell us there are three reasons why people criticize.

1. We criticize to elevate ourselves. The person who has made a failure of himself, who is miserable with his own inadequacies, can strive and struggle and lift himself up, or when he sees those above him, he can convince himself that their success is not genuine and try to pull them down to his level. Criticism says,

"You are not really good at all. You are no better than I, a failure just like myself."

2. We criticize in order to project our miserableness. "Since I am miserable" says the critic, subconsciously, "I'll make you miserable." Something in human nature does, indeed, make misery love company.

3. We criticize the very things of which we are often guilty ourselves or the things which tempt us and trouble us the most. What John tells me about Fred, tells me more about John than it does about Fred. The best way to read a person is to be quiet and hear what he says about others. He will be telling you about himself.

No matter what may be the motive for criticism, the old saying is true, "It doesn't take much size to criticize." The tragic result, however, is that relief from misery gained by projecting miserableness is only temporary. In criticizing, we focus our minds upon negative thoughts, and the mischief that always follows is negative thinking. This only adds to our worries and makes our depression more intense. "Things that thou dost in others see, are the most prevalent in thee."

As the Bible says, "All things are pure," so to the impure are all things impure. Paul scores the sins of criticism, "Thou art inexcusable, O man, whosoever thou art that judgest: for wherein thou judgest another, thou condemnest thyself; for thou that judgest doest the same things."

The matter of dealing with the criticism of others

can be very constructive. First, listen to it objectively. After all, there may be some truth in it. If it is just and honest, do something about it. If it is not, put it out with the other garbage and forget it.

Second, don't try to answer it if it is unjust. If you ignore it, it will die. If it is untrue and you fight it, you will only make it worse. *If you get in a fight with a skunk, you may win, but you will never smell the same.* Don't retaliate against your enemies, turn the other cheek.

The writer of Proverbs says, "Answer not a fool according to his folly, lest thou also be like unto him." If I argue with a fool, he is arguing with one, too.

When Abraham Lincoln was running for President, his opponents circulated a story that he was living in adultery with a Negro woman. What did the great man do? Nothing! Don't defend yourself. Your friends don't need an explanation, and your enemies won't believe it anyway.

Jesus defended his Father; he defended the Word of God; he defended little children; he defended his disciples, but he never defended himself.

Listen to the criticism. If it is honest, benefit from it. If it is unjust, throw it out with the rest of the trash and forget it.

3. Remember that criticism is a compliment in disguise. Nobody ever kicks a dead dog. If some people can't lift themselves up to your success, they will find satisfaction trying to lower you down to their level.

Criticism merely indicates that you have evoked the jealousy of the critic.

The critic is saying, You have done something that I couldn't. I hate you for it. You are above me. You are better than I. I wish I had what you had.

Read through their criticism. See the compliment they are trying to project in their own miserable way.

4. Realize that criticism is the price of success. If you can't stand that consequence of victory, get out of the ball game. It is windy at the top of the ladder. Jesus was the most successful man that ever lived. He was also the most criticized. If you would avoid criticism—say nothing; do nothing; be nothing. He who travels fastest, travels alone.

5. In handling criticism, read, memorize, and practice Matthew 5:43-44. "Ye have heard that it hath been said, Thou shalt love thy neighbour, and hate thine enemy. But I say unto you, Love your enemies, bless them that curse you, do good to them that hate you, and pray for them which despitefully use you, and persecute you." As you love them that hate you, you will find your enemies becoming friends. While it may not change them at first, it will change you. Then they will like the new *you*, and you will like the new *them*. Your worst enemy may become your best friend. He who would have friends, must show himself friendly. A positive attitude and a fixed mind are imperative to positive living. An open, positive, constructive attitude toward criticism is a must.

5

A Positive Mind

"My mind is fixed on thee, O God," said the psalmist. How can a man worry whose mind is fixed on God? How can the spiritual, emotional, and physical problems that develop from worry exist in the life of the man whose total personality has been saturated with a God-presence intoxication? Worry may well be the death of this modern generation. Worry from the cradle to the grave is the great enemy of mankind.

Emotionally upset children, confused teen-agers, are almost as common as their jaded and frustrated parents. A seventeen-year-old boy, who jumped from a ledge in New York City, left this note:

> There's little in taking and giving
> There's little in drinking of wine.
> This living, oh, this living,
>   'Twas never a province of mine.

45

For hard is the battle and sparse is the gain,
   For those who live at the top.
And art is a form of catharsis
   And love is a permanent flop.

And work is the product of cattle,
   And rest for the clam and the shell,
So I'm thinking of throwing the battle,
   Would you kindly direct me to Hell?

What an axiom of modern life that a society which produced the atom bomb, could also produce this. We've conquered outer space, but we cannot conquer inner space.

Medical science is telling us that worry is causing thousands of Americans to contract bone and joint diseases, arthritis, ulcers, and all types of psychosomatic illnesses. If you are beginning to feel stiff around the joints, you had better change your attitude. You may worry yourself into the wheelchair. It is not the work, but the worry that makes the world grow old. That numbers the years of its children; ere half their story is told, that weakens their faith in heaven, and the wisdom of God's great plan. It's not the work, but the worry, that breaks the heart of man.

Years ago, I discovered a wonderful truth. There are only two things worth worrying about in all the world. Think about it for a minute. I am sure you will agree that everything you have ever worried about can be classified under two categories: (1) things you can't change; (2) things you can change.

What could you possibly have to worry about that could not come under these two classifications. *If you can't change it, why worry about it? Why worry yourself into a state of physical and mental exhaustion when with the same physical and mental energy you could develop a concrete course of action and get something done. If it is something you can change, don't worry—get up and change it.* So, there are only two things worth worrying about. Those things you can change and those you can't. If it is something you can change—change it. If you can't change it—forget it. In either case, worry is a waste of time and energy. Worry is paying interest on tomorrow's problems before they happen.

Montaigne, the famous French philosopher said, "My life has been filled with terrible misfortunes, most of which never happened."

As I look back on my life, I believe I can honestly say that three fourths of the things that I feared the most and worried about most sorely, never happened at all. Jesus said it so well in Matthew 6:25-34. "Therefore I say unto you, Take no thought for your life, what ye shall eat, or what ye shall drink; nor yet for your body, what ye shall put on. Is not the life more than meat, and the body than raiment? Behold the fowls of the air: for they sow not, neither do they reap, nor gather into barns; yet your heavenly Father feedeth them. Are ye not much better than they? Which of you by taking thought can add one cubit unto his stature? And why take ye thought for raiment? Consider the lilies of the field, how they grow; they toil not, neither do they spin: and yet I say unto you, That even Solomon in all his glory was not arrayed like one of these. Wherefore, if God so clothe the grass of the field, which today is, and tomorrow is cast into the oven, shall he not much more clothe you, O ye of little faith? Therefore take no thought, saying, What shall we eat? or, What shall we drink, or, Wherewithal shall we be clothed? (For after all these things do the Gentiles seek:) for your heavenly Father knoweth that ye have need of all these things. But seek ye first the kingdom of God, and his righteousness; and all these things shall be added unto you. Take therefore no thought for the morrow: for the morrow shall take thought for the things of itself. Sufficient unto the day is the evil thereof."

The heaviest burdens of life are the burdens of tomorrow that we carry today. Worry is not only useless, weakening, wasting, discouraging, and draining, it is also downright sinful. Worry reveals a lack of faith in God and his Word. He says that his eye is on the sparrow. Worry says, "But you don't see me." He says, "All things work together for good." Worry says, "But not in my life."

The Bible doesn't say all things are good, but it does say all things work together to produce good. There

A Positive Mind

can be no finished product of a beautiful cake without salt and soda, but the salt and soda are not good alone. Working together with the other good ingredients, however, they produce good.

Worry says to God, "I cannot trust you for the salt and soda of life. You may give me too much." "I do not believe you, I do not believe your word, I cannot trust you to properly guide the affairs of my life." Worry is not only useless, it is sinful.

Worry is a robber. It robs you of two of your most valuable assets. The ability to think clearly and to act wisely.

A friend of mine, the young quarterback of one of the nation's leading football teams was having a rough season and had been benched. He could have moaned and groaned, griped and worried himself sick, but he didn't. He remembered that Romans 8:28 was still in the Bible. He benefited from his misfortune, studied his failure, and analyzed his problem. One afternoon the substitute quarterback was injured. Alert and ready to go, he came off the bench, threw four touchdown passes and won the game in seven minutes. Had he worried himself sick, he would have been so physically and emotionally drained that he would have been unable to function properly when the opportunity came. Worry could have robbed him of the important ability to think clearly and act wisely; but it didn't and it need not destroy you.

The solution to worry, as the solution to every problem, is getting Jesus Christ down deep inside your personality. Paul said, "The life which I now live in the flesh I live by the faith of the Son of God." He did not say that his faith was directed toward the Son of God in some spiritual abstract sense, but that he was literally living his physical life, here and now, by the presence of the Son of God in him. In other words, Christ was living in and through him.

Jesus never worried. He was concerned; he was interested. But perfect trust in his Father's ability to do all things well delivered him from worry, even at the death hour. In the midst of adversity, many Christians today are living a life consistently free from worry, because the presence and peace of mind that Christ has personally infused into them through the new birth has made the difference.

One can win over worry by positive thinking. Norman Vincent Peale says, "A positive thinker does not refuse to recognize the negative. He merely refuses to dwell upon it." Philippians 4:6 tells us: "Be careful for nothing; but in every thing by prayer and supplication with thanksgiving let your requests be made known unto God."

Philippians 4:8 continues the same thought—"Finally, brethren, whatsoever things are true, whatsoever things are honest, whatsoever things are just, whatsoever things are pure, whatsoever things are lovely, whatsoever things are of good report; if there be any virtue, and if there be any praise, think on these things."

A Positive Mind

Positive thinking cannot save one, only Christ can do that, but many Christians need to develop a positive mind—free from worry by the truths of these dynamic Scripture passages. Worry can be conquered as one forgets the failures of yesterday and gets started on the opportunities of tomorrow. Paul said it so well, "I press toward the mark for the prize of the high calling of God in Christ Jesus." Yesterday is a canceled check; tomorrow is a promissory note; today is cash in hand. Use it wisely. The person who lives in the past or in the future will never grasp the opportunities of today.

Let the Holy Spirit implant the truth of Matthew 6:33 deep in your soul—"But seek ye first the kingdom of God, and his righteousness; and all these things shall be added unto you."

When Jesus said to seek first the kingdom of God and his righteousness and all of these physical needs of life would be added, he did not mean to totally ignore the reality of modern life, like the little boy in *Mad* magazine with a smile from ear to ear, who says, "Who, me worry?" No, he is saying, I acknowledge my problems; I acknowledge my need; but I also acknowledge that there are things my Heavenly Father can do for me, that I cannot do for myself. Jesus said, "Be of good cheer," or literally, "Cheer up!" "In this world you shall have tribulations, but I have overcome the world." And, "Greater is he that is in you, than he that is in the world." Let him bear your burdens; let him solve your problems, for he is our burden-bearer—yea, he is our peace. He will give you a positive mind. A mind that is stayed on him is free from worry.

6

A Positive Witness

A positive life begins with some positive beginnings and conclusions, some positive habits and attitudes, and a positive conception of keeping and building one's faith. Like a muscle lost from lack of use, or the gift of musical ability lost from lack of practice, faith not strengthened by sharing, may soon be faith that is weakened and lost. Witnessing is the lost art of the twentieth century. "Go" is the forgotten word. "Ye shall be my witnesses," the forgotten commandment. Daily my path is crossed by people from all walks of life. There are full-time religious workers and laymen, men and women, the old and the young. I have discovered in them all a simple secret. The happy ones have in common the happy experience of sharing their faith. In short, they witness for Christ. The ones whose faith remains strong through sharing, are the ones who become well-rounded, well-balanced.

Every denomination has its evangelism program, its layman witness program. We seem to realize the importance of it, and yet we do so very little of it. A positive witness that begins each day with a prayer and a promise, "I shall, this day, share my faith in Christ with some who know him not," will go a long way toward producing a positive and successful day's activities. In St. John, chapter 1, verses 40-42, the Holy Spirit records for us, a wonderful example of witnessing: "One of the two which heard John speak, and followed him, was Andrew, Simon Peter's brother. He first findeth his own brother Simon, and saith unto him, We have found the Messias, which is, being interpreted, the Christ. And he brought him to Jesus." Simple, isn't it? This good man, Andrew, merely found his brother and told him, "Behold, we have found the Messiah." That is witnessing. This is a positive sharing of your faith, telling others who you have found. That seems clear enough and it should be simple enough. Are there any among us that do not believe the story, its importance, its relativity to this day? Hardly so. And yet, the truth is, we don't do much about it. We talk about witnessing, we sing about it, we study and preach it, but the fact is that probably less than 2 percent of Christians actually do verbal, face-to-face witnessing. Why don't we witness? We have found the answer to the problems of the world. We have discovered the healing of the balm of Gilead, and yet, we are silent!

A Positive Witness

What would the world think of one who discovered the cure for cancer and would not share it? What must our Lord think of us? What do we think of ourselves? Why is it so hard to share our faith? Why so difficult to witness? The reasons are simple and the answers too!

1. We do not witness because we don't want to. Obviously simple—yes, but true. The fact of the matter is, we do just about what we please. Few of us are starving to death, because we want to eat. We don't miss many of our favorite TV programs, because we want to see them. Life is a matter of priorities—we do those things that are important to us. Talk to some people about money matters, the stock market, and high finance, and watch their eyes light up. This is where there interest lies. This is what they like. But they could not be less interested in sharing their faith in Christ. They just don't care. We just don't want to—why? Perhaps it could be embarrassing. Perhaps we have no faith to share. Many are unconverted themselves and simply have nothing to tell. If there is an inability to witness, there is a genuine possibility that one *has* nothing to witness to, and his salvation experience should be reconsidered, as he may not be a Christian at all. He may simply have no faith to share. Then, he may have no religion to wear.

What about the man we stand next to at work all day? What about the man in the office that has heard our profanity? Suppose we got a prospect card with his name on it? Suppose I am called upon to visit him! How embarrassed to stand face to face with one that knows the inconsistency of my life and attempt to witness for Christ. "It may be that our religion is showing." If this is true of you, repent of your sins and rededicate your life this very moment to Christ. Why don't we witness? Why don't we want to? Because we have nothing to share, nothing to wear and oftentimes because we simply have no heart to care. We really couldn't care less if anyone were saved at all.

Wouldn't it be wonderful if Christian people cared so for lost souls that they could not rest until they had witnessed, until they had daily shared their faith? I hear some say, "If I had such compassion, I would go." "I wish with all my heart I did have it so I could make myself go." But wait, you have the order reversed. The reason you do not have compassion is because you have not gone. When you become involved with unsaved people, when you go to them and see their needs, their problems, and tell them of Christ, then you will get a burden for them. Then you will have concern and you will rejoice at their conversion. Then you will become a witness and a soul-winner. Don't wait until you get compassion to go. Start witnessing now, become involved in the needs and burdens of others and you will become compassionate.

2. But there is a second reason why we do not witness. Not only do we not care, but also, we simply do not know how to witness. And so, we have a soul-winning

A Positive Witness

course. We read study course books, take a few lessons on "How to do it," and then we are supposed to be soul-winners. Many Christians have their walls lined with award seals for study course books on "how to win souls" and are supposed to know how to do it; but though they have won a seal, most have never won a soul.

The average study course book on soul-winning may have ten or fifteen chapters on how to win the Communist, how to win the Buddhist, how to win the atheist, the agnostic, and others. At the bottom of each of these chapters will be ten verses of Scriptures that we are supposed to memorize. That means 150 verses before we even begin, and most of us can't even remember our ZIP Code.

The first chapter usually begins by listing the qualifications of a soul-winner that are so demanding they even make me want to quit before I begin.

On the surface, the fact that I do not know how to witness seems to be a just reason for not witnessing, but in reality, that is not the case at all. And so, now we come to it. Why don't we share our faith? Why do we find it so hard to witness? Because we do not want to? Because we do not know how? Yes, but the real reason is much deeper. It is obvious from St. John's story that we simply don't know what witnessing really is!

Listen again to the exciting record of Andrew witnessing to Peter in verse 41, "He first findeth his own brother Simon." Now stop a minute. What did Andrew do? He obviously located one that he loved. Is this witnessing? No, it is visiting. Visiting is good, visiting is important—but visiting is not witnessing!

Sometimes I preach in churches that report sixteen hundred visits through the Sunday School and my heart leaps for joy. Sixteen hundred witnessing for Christ. Surely five hundred will come down in the opening night of the revival, but no one comes. The reason is obvious. The people have visited, but they have not witnessed. It is not difficult in these days to find one's brother. It is not hard to visit. The average pastor can locate anyone in his city within thirty minutes, but so what?

Door-to-door salesmen visit; insurance men visit; everyone visits. You can hire people to visit, but visiting is not witnessing. The devil has certainly defeated us at this point. In the average church, many visits are made, but little witnessing for Jesus is done. We talk about the church building and we invite them to visit and we tell them what a great preacher we have. They are visited in the name of the church, but they never hear about Jesus. Why don't we witness? Because we don't know what witnessing is.

Witnessing is not visiting. Witnessing is not finding one's brother. Second, witnessing is not soul-winning. Witnessing should precede soul-winning. Presenting the four spiritual laws, giving out tracts, or asking someone if he is saved is fine. It is important. It is

A Positive Witness

the result of the witness, it should follow the witness, but it is not witnessing.

Look again at the text. He found his brother, Simon, and he said unto him, "We have found the Messiah." That is witnessing. Visiting is an avenue that leads you to the person to whom you can witness. Visiting is finding your brother. Witnessing is telling him what you have found. Soul-winning is telling him how he can find it. All three are important, but the first and last, without the second, visiting, and soul-winning without the personal testimony, the personal witness of the soul-winner, may produce a shallow type of convert and produce less results.

Many people these days are trying to make winning people to Jesus easy. You can get on the elevator at the first floor and get somebody to nod his head yes to four questions and win him to Christ by the tenth floor. But real soul-winning takes time. There must be love and compassion. There must be repentance.

Visiting is finding your brother. Witnessing is telling your brother what you have found. Soul-winning is explaining to your brother a plan by which he may find the same thing. Don't leave out the witness.

Confused, neurotic, frustrated Christians seem to be the order of the day. But never do I find such people among faithful witnesses for Christ. The one who has learned to build his faith by sharing his faith will quickly become a fully matured Christian, able to cope with life's temptations and tribulations, its defeats, as well as its victories. What an example Andrew has given us. We can do it too.

Remember, visiting is finding your brother. Witnessing is telling him what you have found. Soul-winning is telling him how to find it.

Witnessing is not arguing theology; it is not preaching sermons; it is not giving your ideas about religion. If you know Jesus, you can never keep your faith better, than by giving it away. Witnessing tells what you know. "Behold, I have found the Messiah." John recorded it and Andrew did it so well. "Go thou and do likewise."

Gateway Seminary Library